CONTENTS

INTRODUCTION

The *Top Gear* annual is packed with so many cool cars, epic puzzles, fun facts and so much crazy TV action that you may need to lie down and recover in a dark room after reading it! Just don't read it in a dark room, because then you won't see any of the pages and the words and the pictures. That would be silly, which is actually a bit like the stuff inside this book. Er, let's get our engines started and move on, shall we?

Chris Evans

THE ONE THAT . . . has ginger hair, jumps around the studio, wears leather jackets and LOVES going 200 mph in a McLaren 675LT on the *Top Gear* track.

MOST LIKELY TO . . . shout 'Aarrgghh!' behind the wheel of a supercar. Oh, and feel a bit unwell in the passenger seat while Sabine is driving. Or while Jenson Button is driving.

Matt LeBlanc

THE ONE THAT . . . talks like an American, gets other Americans on the show and wears a Stars and Stripes helmet. We're beginning to think Matt may actually be an American . . .

MOST LIKELY TO . . . blast around in off-roaders like the Ariel Nomad, Jaguar F-Pace and Willy's Jeep. And say American things like 'go figure' and 'you do the math'.

Eddie Jordan

THE ONE THAT . . . used to own a Formula One team and now treats ordinary cars, like a Mercedes GLC, like it is an F1 car. Matt says he struggles to understand what Eddie is talking about. Eddie likes to talk a lot!

MOST LIKELY TO . . . cheat during a *Top Gear* challenge and to cause bits of his car to fall off! Eddie is *not* the best off-road driver in the world, in all honesty. But remember he used to have an F1 team, which makes him super cool!

WELCOME TO TOP GEAR!

BBC Children's Books are published by Puffin Books,
part of the Penguin Random House group of companies
whose addresses can be found at global.penguinrandomhouse.com.
www.penguin.co.uk   www.puffin.co.uk   www.ladybird.co.uk

First published 2016
Written by Kevin Pettman and Dan Newman.
Illustrations pp. 6-7 and pp. 30-33 by Dan Lewis
Lorrygami origami by Crease Lightning Ltd

Printed in Italy   001
ISBN: 978-1-405-92824-3

Picture credits: All photos © BBC Worldwide except the following – Alamy: Jack Sullivan p. 51 (Caparo T1). Shutterstock: benchart p. 17 (seagull),
Eric Isselee p. 38 (dog), fixelhouse p. 38 (TV), Keith Homan p. 38 (Xbox), kolopach pp. 28-29 (cars), Maksym Bondarchuk p. 20 (headphones), Natursports
p. 38 (Luis Suarez), Orlok p. 28 (VW Golf), PaulPaladin p. 20 (cards), Rodrigo Garrido p. 37 (Defender jumping), Snap2Art p. 37 (Defender in water).

Sabine Schmitz

THE ONE THAT . . . is a lady and comes from Germany. A German lady, if you will! Sabine has been racing cars since before she could walk. Probably.

MOST LIKELY TO . . . make her passenger feel a bit unwell, whether that's Chris Evans or a top US fighter pilot. You see, Sabine is a very quick and very talented driver and is right at home behind the wheel of a Corvette Z06 or an Audi R8 V10 Plus.

Rory Reid

THE ONE THAT . . . is a bit cheeky, a bit south-Londony and a bit happy blasting the Ford Focus RS hot hatch around roads in Wales. Nice one, Rory!

MOST LIKELY TO . . . talk a lot about cars and ask lots of questions about cars, especially if he knows it might wind Chris Harris up a little bit!

Chris Harris

THE ONE THAT . . . does lots of wheel spins in the Aston Martin Vulcan and drives the mega awesome Ferrari F12tdf in France! No surprise that Chris Harris smiles a lot in both these events.

MOST LIKELY TO . . . get into a bit of an argument with Rory Reid about stupid cars. Chris likes proper cars and driving them proper fast on a proper track.

The Stig

THE ONE THAT . . . doesn't say anything and only ever wears a white racing suit. Lives at the *Top Gear* track (we think).

MOST LIKELY TO . . . drive any car, or any vehicle to come think of it, very quickly. The tame racing driver is only interested in bhp, down force, gear ratios and torque. Definitely not interested in flower arranging and *The Great British Bake Off.*

CHALLENGE GENERATOR

Just how do you put a bonkers TV show like *Top Gear* together? It's not easy! Firstly, days are ~~wasted arguing~~ spent discussing ideas.
Then it takes hours and hours to ~~cobble something together quickly~~ research and craft the components.
Or, we could use something like this . . .

Roll a dice and use our game to create the ultimate *Top Gear* challenge.

A ROLL A DICE!

B ROLL AGAIN!

C ROLL AGAIN!

WE WERE GIVEN A . . .

1 = muscle car

2 = Jeep

3 = Land Rover

4 = two-seater sports car

5 = three-wheeler

6 = Limousine

WE WERE THEN CHALLENGED TO . . .

1 = race 965 miles to Venice

2 = blast around a Moroccan desert

3 = race an Aston Martin in Abu Dhabi

4 = be a wedding chauffeur

5 = do a tour of London

6 = blitz the Mazda Raceway Laguna Seca in California

AND WE MET . . .

1 = a pop star

2 = a Formula One driver

3 = a triathlete

4 = a New Yorker

5 = a sick bag

6 = Ken Block

E ROLL AGAIN!

BUT SOMEHOW, WE ALSO . . .

1 = met some scary American footballers

2 = cooked while driving

3 = raced the Orient Express

4 = did a very, very, very big wheel spin

5 = had a laser tracker (that looked like a machine gun) stuck to our car's roof

6 = threw up

F ROLL AGAIN!

BUT WE DID GET TO DRIVE A . . .

1 = Ferrari F12tdf

2 = McLaren 675 LT

3 = Aston Martin Vulcan

4 = Rolls Royce Dawn

5 = Ford Mustang

6 = Audi R8 V10 Plus

D ROLL AGAIN!

THEN WE SET OFF TO . . .

1 = drive to Blackpool

2 = drive to the Arc de Triomphe

3 = drive around Wales

4 = drive up a huuuge hill

5 = drive up a huuuge African mountain

6 = drive our co-presenters crazy

DRAW YOUR OWN TOP GEAR

You're not usually allowed to draw on books. Unless it's a drawing book, in which case it's positively encouraged! Well, in this *Top Gear* book we encourage you to draw your own *Top Gear* studio, cars and presenter. There's even a big space below to make it easy for you. So grab a pen or pencil and get scribblin'!

Big American flag to make Matt happy?

Draw a cool car here.

on lights visible from Mars?

Giant Stig statue on the roof?

Now turn to page 56 to create your own *Top Gear* track . . .

DRESS THE STIG

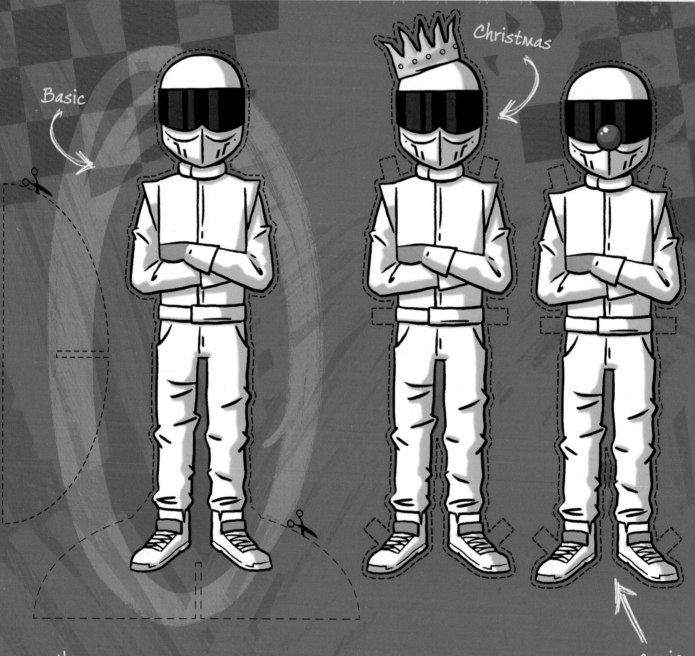

Basic

Christmas

Comic Relief

25th November*

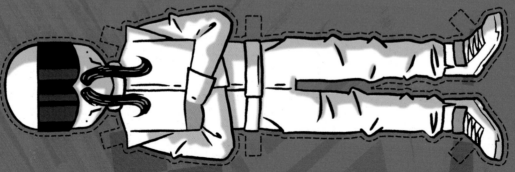

*The birthday of Karl Benz, the inventor of the motor car. Worth celebrating.

The tame racing driver always looks the same . . . or does he? We already know his cousins around the world dress slightly differently. So perhaps the Stig has some special outfits tucked away for special occasions? Cut out these variations on the basic version and imagine the possibilities!

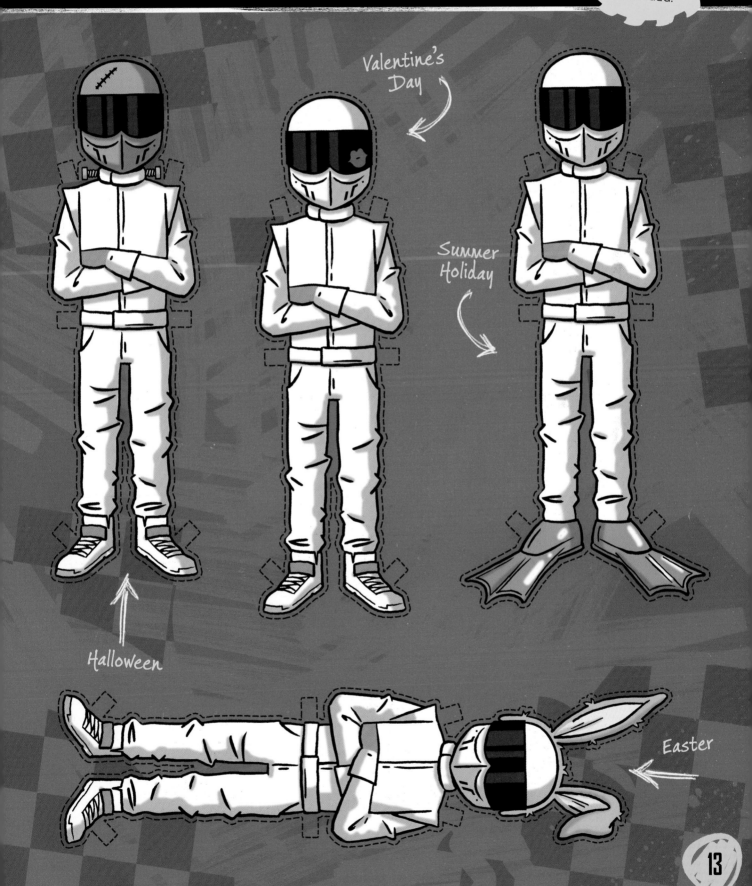

Valentine's Day

Summer Holiday

Halloween

Easter

13

WHICH CAR HAS 🙂 THE HAPPIEST FACE?

Apparently some carmakers deliberately try to make it look as if their cars have faces (while others definitely don't). The Mini Paceman, for instance, looks a bit sad. That got us thinking. Are there any happy cars out there? Draw some faces on these and see what you think!

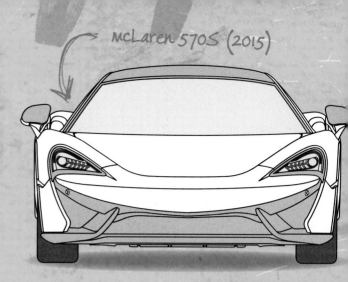
McLaren 570S (2015)

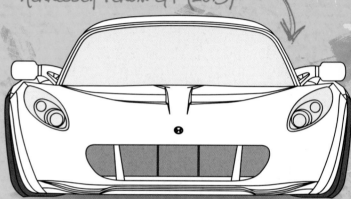
Hennessey Venom GT (2013)

VW Up! (2012)

M·GW 9274

Trabant 601 (1963)

Honda NSX (2015)

Ferrari California (2010)

Vauxhall Adam (2013)

Maserati Gran Turismo (2009)

Honda Brio (2012)

Lotus Elise (2002)

Suzuki Alto (2009)

Mazda 3 (2010)

15

UK vs USA

What do you get if you put Chris Evans, Matt LeBlanc, two Reliant Rialtos, a Land Rover Series 1, a Willy's Jeep and a load of rain, mud, sand and ice creams together? The *Top Gear* UK vs USA challenge, that's what!

> Nice wheels, Matt. Great paintjob!

> Yours is nicer!

C850 YBK

YFR 385Y

DAY 1

Chris and Matt set off from central London to drive 250 miles north to Blackpool in their convertible Reliant Rialtos.

But just 26 miles from London, Matt's mighty three-wheeled motor is struggling. But he doesn't want to let Team America down . . .

> Our very first *Top Gear* road trip!

> Let's roll!

C850 YBK

SSSSSSSSSSSSSSSSS

YFR 385Y

> It's just overheating. It's not oil smoke.

Reliant Rialto stats

Engine: 850 cc
Power: 40 bhp *(if you're lucky)*
Top speed: 85 mph *(what, down a hill?)*
Value today: £243.27

Back on the M40, Matt thinks (well, hopes) they are nearing their destination . . .

C850 YBK

I just saw a sign for Oxford. Does that mean we're near Blackpool?

It's now raining and much colder. I'm dressed like Captain Birdseye. Matt is dressed like a bear.

Not really. We're half the country away still.

I'm going to have a good long talk with the wardrobe department. With a stick!

Just a few miles later, Matt has to pull off the motorway again to tend to his poorly little car.

Do I *look* happy?

Chris's imagination starts to go a bit crazy . . .

Ha, ha!

My wiper is imitating the sound of a seagull at the seaside!

Matt decides he needs some help, from a tow truck. At last he's on the move.

Heroically, or stupidly, Matt decides to drive the last ten miles to Blackpool. Will his Rialto make it that far though?

I'm not stopping again. I'm gonna go until it blows up!

Drives itself this thing, really.

Still 200 miles from Blackpool

Hold it together – about 500 metres!

North of Birmingham, the weather gets a tad chilly for Chris and Matt!

Alright! We made it!

Chris's Land Rover Series 1
Nationality: British
Engine: 1.6-litre petrol
Power: 50 bhp

Now we're talking. Two legends!

This is now proper USA against UK.

Matt's Willy's Jeep
Nationality: American
Engine: 2.2-litre diesel
Power: 70 bhp

DAY 2

The next day, Chris and Matt meet at Blackpool beach and are given two new vehicles for the day's challenges.

First challenge is a speed test. One kilometre run-up and fastest through the timing gate.

Piece of cake! Feel that American power, baby!

SCORE: USA 1 UK 0

Matt clocks the fastest speed – 48 mph compared to Chris's 43.1 mph.

The next challenge is a tug of war. Chris is helped by local rugby players and Matt has the beef of some American footballers.

Come on, boys!

But the only victor is the sand and no winner is declared.

SCORE: USA 1 UK 0

Next is a triple-drag challenge. The *Top Gear* presenters have a drag race to the sea, then drag an ice-cream van from the water before picking up a drag queen and racing to the finish line.

Oh no! The American's got the lead!

See you later!

Matt is first to finish after picking up his drag queen and racing back across Blackpool beach.

SCORE: USA 2 UK 0

Here we go! Yeah!

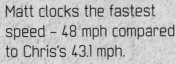

DAY 3

"Yeah! The Reliants are back!"

"Er, yay."

"Soon the Americans' path is blocked, but that's no bother when Nick has the muscle to clear the road!"

"It's good to have strong friends."

"Grrr!"

Matt's 2-0 lead gives him a one-second head start in the deciding challenge, a race up Muncaster Fell in the Lake District . . . towing their Reliant Rialtos as their 'flags'.

American strongman Nick Best arrives to help Matt reach the top of the hill first.

"It's neck and neck, until Matt gives Chris a 'friendly' tap with his Jeep!"

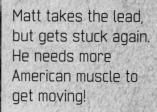

"KKRASSH!"

"Keep checking the Reliant is still there!"

"Everything."

"How much do you lift?"

"Give me a push, Nick!"

"Matt takes the lead, but gets stuck again. He needs more American muscle to get moving!"

"But Chris has help from British triathlon legend, Alistair Brownlee."

Athlete stats

Nick Best, strongman	Alistair Brownlee, triathlete
Height: 6 ft 2 ins	**Height:** 6 ft
Weight: 143 kg	**Weight:** 70 kg

Team America and Team Britain set off in a race to pull the Rialtos up the muddy terrain.

"Alistair's brother, Jonathan, appears and takes the door off. Chris thinks he'll win if he takes just this bit of the car to the top of the hill."

"Yeeeaahhh!"

"But you didn't bring enough of the car!"

"Think we're still on the right route here!"

The teams split up – Chris takes a clear route but Matt sees a shortcut across a bumpy track.

"I *may* have cheated . . ."

SCORE: UK wins!

(kind of!)

Are We There Yet!?!

Top Gear loves cars. (Obviously!) But we don't like being stuck in them for ages, on a long and dull journey or in bumper-to-bumper traffic on the M6. This is when all cars become b-o-o-o-ring! So here, *Top Gear* offers advice on how you can liven up those endless and mind-numbingly boring journeys.

NOT VERY USEFUL *TG* ADVICE

- Try out all the gadgets fitted in your car. Unless you're in a twelve-year-old Fiat Punto, because then the level of gadgetry will be zero.
- Look at the view. This may not be very exciting.
- Eat the sun visors/seats if you are a dog
- Learn a foreign language. Use your new skills to buy local food from roadside stalls.
- Learn how to play a musical instrument
- Learn magic tricks involving doves
- Break your journey at 'interesting' local sights. If you're near Blackpool, *Top Gear* recommends the pier. But don't drive on it, please.

MORE USEFUL ADVICE

Prepare

- Get enough sleep before setting off
- Clean the car – or your seat, at least
- Charge the batteries on your devices
- Dress comfortably

Come on, you beauty!

871 YUA

Pack

- Headphones
- Colouring books
- Devices
- Games – magnetic travel ones or a pack of cards
- Something to read
- Sweets that take a while to eat and aren't messy
- A pillow or blanket if you want to nap
- Refillable water bottle
- Dry-wipe markers to draw on the windows. Don't use permanent ones!

DO
Talk to each other
Stop regularly
Go to the loo when you stop
Chill out

DON'T
Eat salty foods, which will make you thirsty!
Eat chocolate if the car gets warm!
Argue or fight. There's nowhere to go!
Drink too much, or too fast – you'll need to wee!

CLASSIC CAR GAMES

I-Spy
One player secretly chooses an item in the vehicle. Everyone else takes turn guessing what the item is.

Name That Tune
Each time a new song comes on the radio, the first person to name it gets a point.

Twenty Questions
One player thinks of an object. The others ask 'yes' or 'no' questions trying to guess the item before they reach 20 'no's.

ABCs
Pick a category (movies, animals, etc.) and go around in circles giving examples that start with consecutive letters of the alphabet.

Storytelling
Someone tells the first sentence of a story. The next person tells the next sentence, and so on. Try to make it as funny as possible.

Two Truths and a Lie
Each person tells two true facts about themselves and one lie. The others must guess which is false.

Would You Rather?
Give two unlikely scenarios and make each passenger say which one they'd rather do.

Top Gear likes a desert. Matt had awesome fun maxing out an Ariel Nomad on the sands of Morocco, for example. But there is a lot of room in the desert, nothing to run into and it can be quite tricky to know which way to point your car. Recreate the experience for yourself with this fun – and frustrating – game . . .

1 The youngest player starts first, from the centre space.

2 Whenever it's your turn, roll the dice once to decide which direction to go. Use the compass icon in the centre to guide you. The number you roll dictates the direction you head in.

3 Roll again to decide how many spaces you'll go in that direction:
Roll 1 or 2 = move one space
Roll 3 or 4 = move two spaces
Roll 5 or 6 = move three spaces.

4 Play rotates clockwise. If your move would mean landing on top of another player, stop behind them.

5 The winner is the first player to reach the road at the edge of the desert.

You will need
Counters
A dice

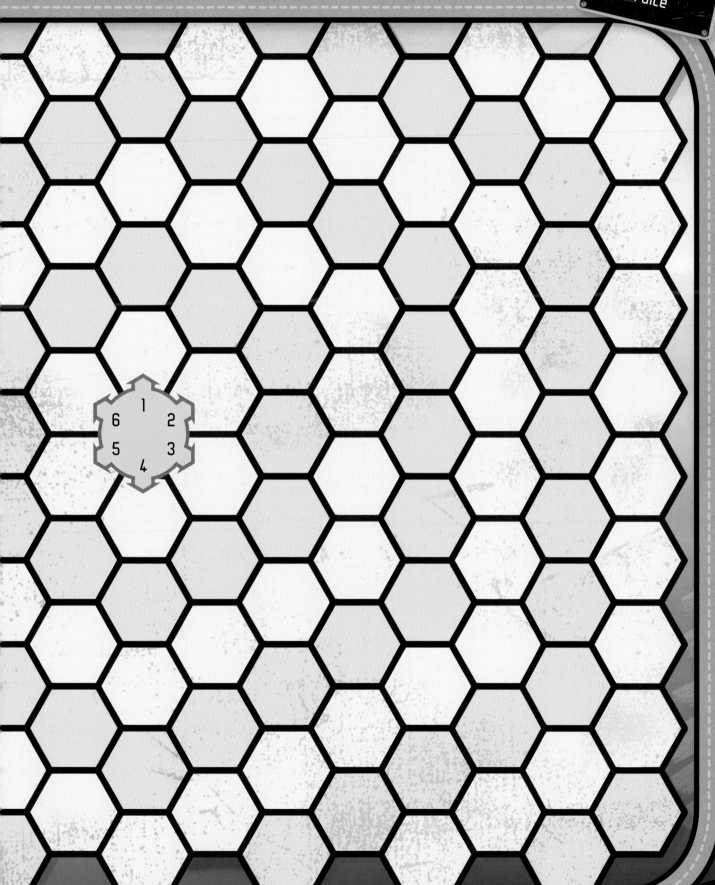

HOT HATCH

Hatchbacks are the best cars in the world! They're small, practical, family friendly and cheap. But how do you turn a normal, boring hatch into a hilarious hot hatch? *Top Gear* reveals what you need . . .

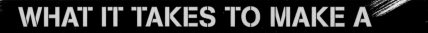

SPEED

A good hot hatch should do zero to 60 mph in under seven seconds. A great one can crack it in less than five seconds and max out at over 150 mph. That'll put some sports cars to shame.

PRICE

Expect to pay between £20,000 to £30,000 for a decent hot hatch, which could be twice what you'd pay for a rubbish one. But the extra cash will be worth it for the big smile something like a Honda Civic Type R will put on your chops!

LOOKS

A hot hatch must stand out from the crowd. A body kit, spoiler, diffuser, fancy paint job with stickers and tinted windows will tick that box. Look at this one on the Civic.

My fave is the Focus RS!

Mercedes AMG A45   Ford Focus RS   Honda Civic Type R

Ford Focus RS

Power: 345 bhp
0-60 mph: 4.7 seconds
Top speed: 165 mph
Price: £29,995

SPACE

A hot hatch needs to have a boot with room for more than just your pencil case. It will have rear seats, cup holders and a glove box. Your pencil case will fit neatly in there.

ENGINE

A hot hatch's engine will usually be a 2.0-litre four-cylinder turbo, cranking out more than 200 bhp. Some, like the Audi RS3, will have a 2.5-litre engine and more than 350 bhp. Bonkers.

TYRES

Small and skinny, so that they slide around a Tesco car park on a Tuesday or a track day event on a Sunday.

NOISE

Hot hatches dish out the decibels a bit more than a Nissan Leaf, thanks to their rev-tastic engines and sporty exhausts. The Audi S1 actually has four exhausts, which is really just being greedy.

WEIGHT

The lighter a hot hatch is, the quicker it will go. Some will have a roll cage instead of rear seats, which means mum and dad can't take you anywhere. Which also saves weight.

TOP GEAR DOES TOP GUN

Top Gear becomes *Top Gun* as Chris and Sabine battle in American speed machines at a US Naval Air Station. With laser-tracking guns strapped to their roofs, of course!

Inside their muscle cars, Chris and Sabine are joined by US Naval pilots who are in charge of the laser gun on top of the car. The first to get a missile lock on the other car wins.

Which is the king of muscle cars? Viper or 'Vette?

Sabine's Chevrolet Corvette Z06

Power: 650 bhp
0-60 mph: 3.8 seconds
Top speed: 199 mph
Engine: 6.2-litre V8
Price: £67,331

Ginger! I don't like you because you're dangerous.

Chris's Dodge Viper ACR

Power: 645 bhp
0-60 mph: 3.5 seconds
Engine: 8.4-litre V10
Top speed: 177 mph
Price: £85,000

Chris's superior acceleration puts him in front, but the Viper's huge rear wing actually slows it down in the straights.

The Viper's wing is doing its thing!

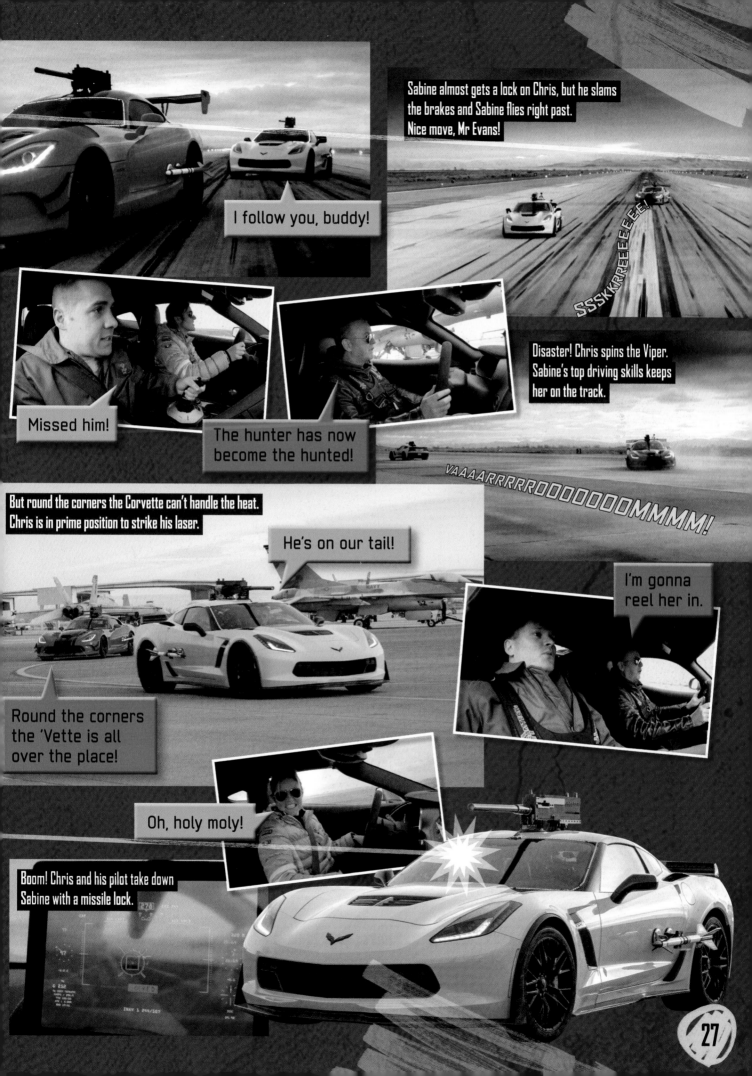

WHAT DO WE ACTUALLY DRIVE?

Top Gear likes to blitz around our track in £300,000 supercars or blast multimillion-pound Aston Martins on circuits in Abu Dhabi. But, deep down, we know this isn't a normal driving experience for most people in the UK. We know that a Ferrari or a Pagani is not a common sight on the school run or commuter drive. So, we've looked at some spreadsheets and graphs to work out which cars are *actually* driven and bought in the UK.

WARNING: normal cars are on these pages!

(well . . . just one)

There are 4.4 million Fords driving around Britain.

There are 31.1 million cars on UK roads.

The top German car in the UK is the VW Golf, with 1.04 million on our streets.

MOST POPULAR COLOURS FOR NEW CARS

White 564,393

Black 509,677

Grey 411,717

Blue 386,432

Red 318,897

MOST POPULAR MODELS IN 2015

FORD FIESTA	VW POLO
VAUXHALL CORSA	VAUXHALL ASTRA
FORD FOCUS	AUDI A3
VW GOLF	MINI
NISSAN QASHQAI	VAUXHALL MOKA

2015 NEW CARS BY MANUFACTURER

Manufacturer	Sales
FORD	335,267
VAUXHALL	269,766
VOLKSWAGEN	223,784
BMW	167,391
AUDI	166,709
NISSAN	153,937
MERCEDES-BENZ	145,254
PEUGEOT	104,249
TOYOTA	98,709
HYUNDAI	88,117
KIA	78,489
RENAULT	75,618
SKODA	74,692
CITROËN	68,811
LAND ROVER	66,574
FIAT	64,257
HONDA	53,417
SEAT	47,654
MAZDA	45,504
VOLVO	43,432
SUZUKI	34,437
DACIA	26,228
JAGUAR	23,954
MITSUBISHI	22,693
DS	19,815
LEXUS	13,269
PORSCHE	12,167
JEEP	10,794
SMART	8,455
ALFA ROMEO	5,069
SUBARU	3,455
SSANGYONG	3,344
MG	3,152
ABARTH	2,743
MASERATI	1,434
BENTLEY	1,379
TESLA	1,221
INFINITI	1,195
ASTON MARTIN	949

2015 EUROPEAN SALES OF 'EXOTIC' CARS

Car	Sales
BENTLEY CONTINENTAL GT	1,631
FERRARI 458 ITALIA	934
LAMBORGHINI HURACÁN	502
ASTON MARTIN VANQUISH	365
ASTON MARTIN DB9	315
FERRARI F12	290
LAMBORGHINI AVENTADOR	250
ROLLS ROYCE WRAITH	242
FERRARI 488	212
FERRARI FF	153
MERCEDES-BENZ SLS AMG	56
BUGATTI VEYRON	12
LAMBORGHINI GALLARDO	12

Source: Bart Demandt, left-lane.com

LORRYGAMI

Red lorry, yellow lorry.
Red lorry, yellow lorry.
Which will you make?

You will need
- 24 cm square of thin paper with one coloured side
- Steady hands
- Lots of patience

Key

Valley fold – towards you

- - - - - - - - - -

Mountain fold – away from you

Fold and unfold

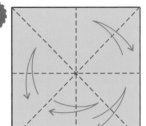

1 Fold and unfold the square lengthwise and diagonally through the middle.

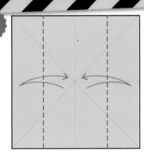

2 Fold and unfold the outer edges to the middle.

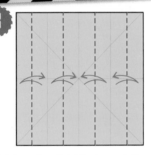

3 Fold and unfold between the creases just made, dividing the square into eight sections.

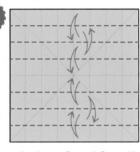

4 Repeat steps 2 and 3 on the other axis, dividing it into 64 squares.

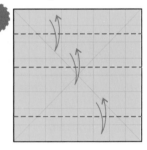

5 Fold and unfold three times using the creases as guides then turn over left to right.

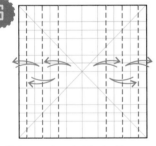

6 Fold and unfold six times as shown.

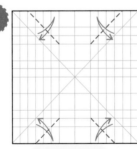

7 Fold and unfold four guide creases as shown. Then turn over.

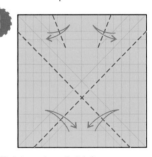

8 Fold and unfold four more guide creases as shown.

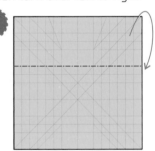

9 Fold the upper section behind, along the fourth crease from the upper edge.

10 Fold and unfold the top right corner.

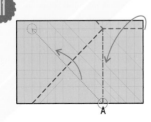

11 Make these folds carefully to move point A up to the left and the back layer out to the right.

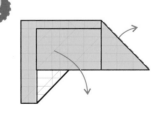

12 Unfold the model back to step 10.

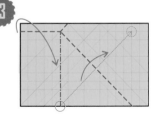

13 Repeat steps 10 to 12 on the left side. Unfold the model back to step 9 to make a square.

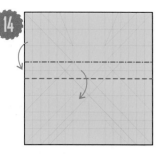

14

Fold the creases shown 90° to make a zig zag or step.

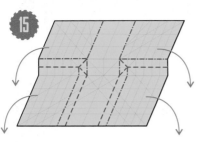

15

Fold the sides down. At the same time pinch the 'step' and refold steps 10 to 13 on both sides.

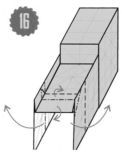

16

Fold the edges out on both sides. The edge nearest you will fold down and flatten.

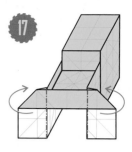

17

Fold back the flaps shown on both sides.

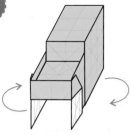

18

Turn the model round to work on the front of the lorry.

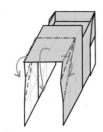

19

Fold the upper edge down 45°. At the same time fold the sides in along the creases made in steps 7 and 8.

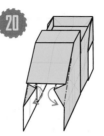

20

Fold the inner edges down so they are flat against the insides.

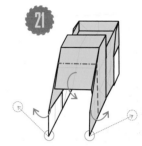

21

Fold the sides out 90°, the top edge will fold down at the same time.

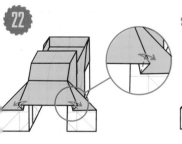

22

Fold and unfold these small corners on both sides.

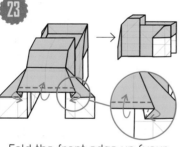

23

Fold the front edge up (your fold should line up with the third crease down).

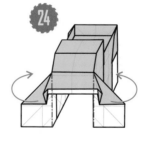

24

Fold both front flaps back so they are flat against the sides.

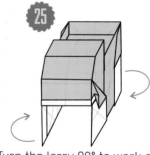

25

Turn the lorry 90° to work on the side.

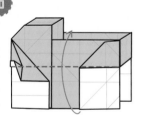

26

Fold the side up.

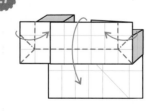

27

Fold the top edge down (along the second crease). At the same time, fold the sides in.

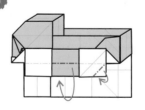

28

Fold the bottom edge behind and into the model. At the same time fold the right corner back as shown.

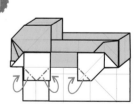

29

Fold the corners shown behind and into the model.

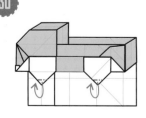

30

Fold the bottom of the wheels behind and into the model.

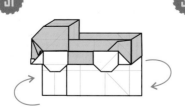

31

Turn the model round to work on the other side of the lorry.

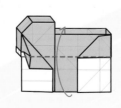

32

Repeat steps 26 to 30.

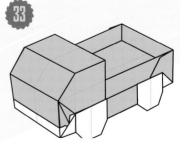

33

Your lorry is complete! Now make another in a different colour.

Aston Martin Vulcan

HURACÁN OR HUAYRA?

The car has been around for over 100 years now, and it seems like there's beginning to be a problem: carmakers are running out of cool names. Cars used to be called things like 'Firebird' or 'Javelin'. Nowadays. . . how do you even say 'Huayra'? Test your knowledge by drawing lines to match each make to the right model. They're not all current models, but they are all genuine.

Roomster   KIA   Vaneo   MITSUBISHI   Cube   PROTON

SUZUKI   Freed Spike   FORD   Cactus   VOLKSWAGEN   Adam Slam

Toppo Guppy   HONDA   Wind   SKODA   Probe   MERCEDES

ISUZU   Savvy   TOYOTA   CITROËN   Wagon R   NISSAN

Routan   FIAT   Accent   Ulysse   VAUXHALL   pro_cee'd

RENAULT   Chaser Lordly   MAZDA   Bongo Friendee   Bighorn Plaisir   HYUNDAI

33

SUPERCAR

Let's face it, none of us are ever going to be able to afford
a supercar. But that doesn't mean you can't have one.
No, that doesn't mean steal one, silly. MAKE one!

1. Photocopy these pages to double size. This way, you can keep these pages for reference.

2. Carefully cut out the car pieces along the solid outlines and assemble them in number order. (Piece 1, piece 2 etc.)

3. Score along dotted and dashed lines using closed scissors.

4. Fold all the scored lines: dotted lines fold towards you, dashed lines fold away.

5. Glue the flaps in alphabetical order. (It should be obvious where unlabelled flaps go.) Let the glue dry.

6. When you've assembled parts 1–6, stick 7 and 9 to 8. Stick the body on to the base, starting at the front and gently bending to fit.

7. Glue each tyre into a ring, then fold and glue a cross on each side. Stick an alloy on to both sides of each tyre. Stick the wheels on the base.

8. Use coloured pens to touch up any white patches on the corners and edges.

9. Push around your desktop making 'RRRRUUURRR' noises.

WARNING

Do not attempt this if your practical skills are poor. You will need PVA glue, a small paintbrush, small scissors, patience, a ruler, steady hands and NO HAMMERS AT ALL.

Cut lines ⋯⋯⋯⋯ Fold up lines
Fold down lines ━━━ Lines on bodywork

F H

D
5
S
U
L
M

1
A
B

J
4
K
T
C
R

C
3
P
B
Q
D
G
I

9

O

N

7

Back wheels (thicker)   Front wheels (thinner)

Folding the wheels

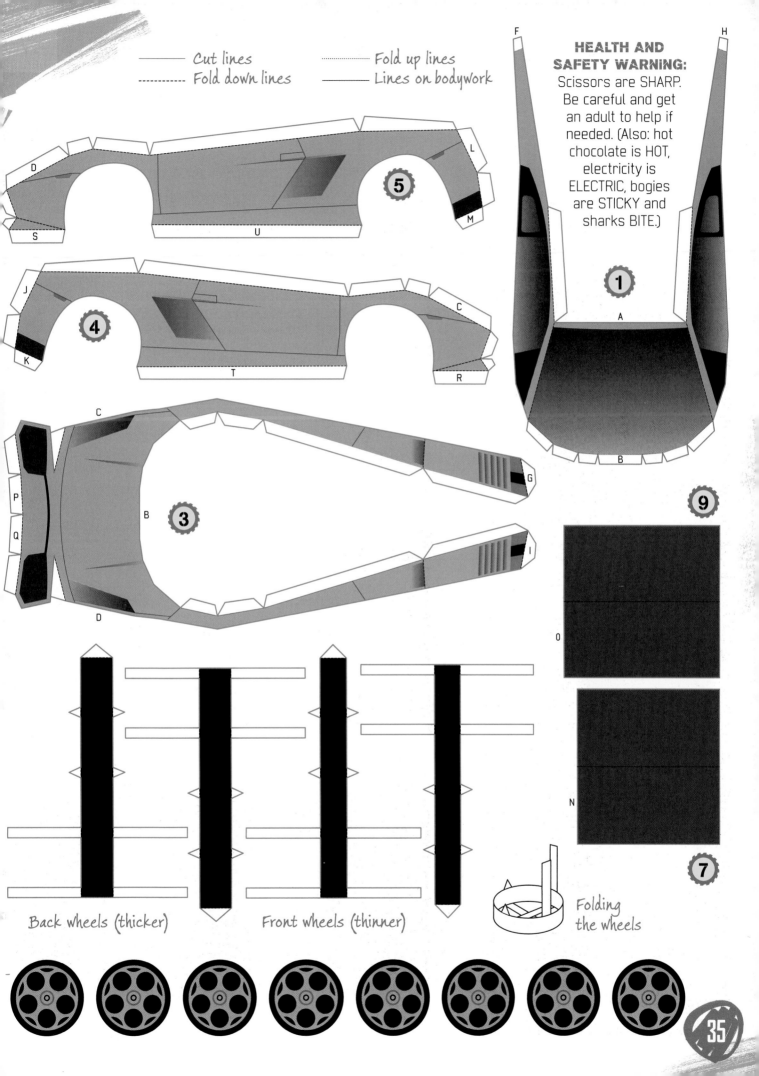

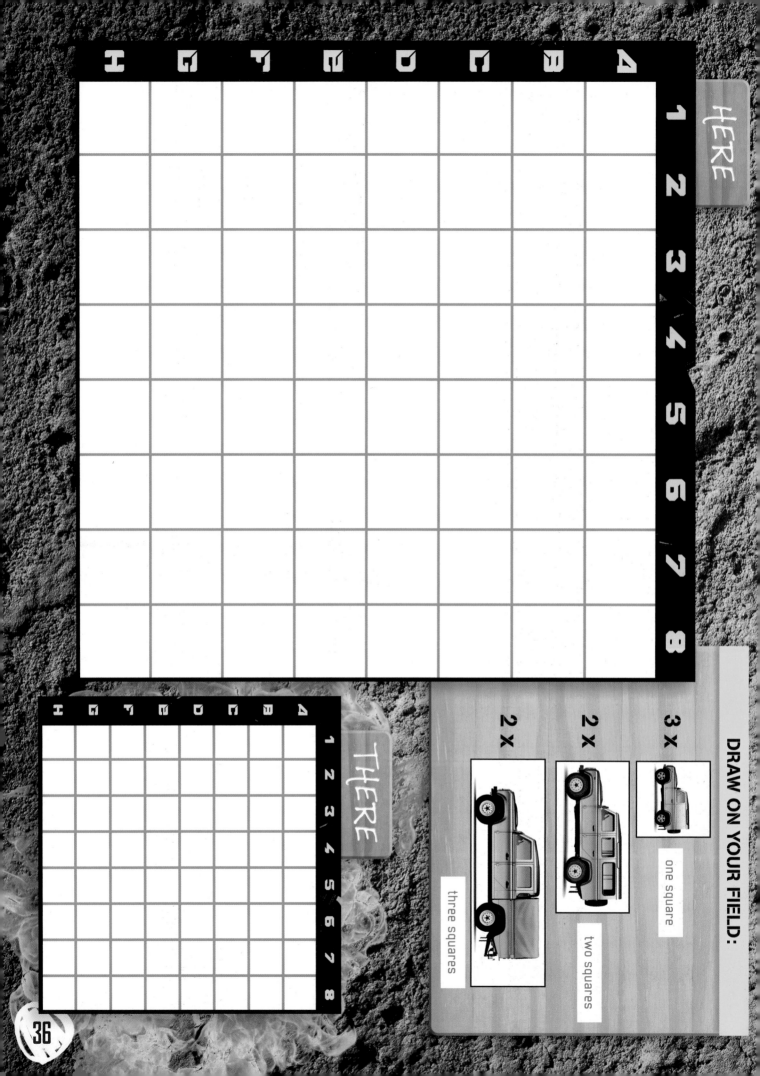

YOU DESTROYED MY DEFENDER

HOW TO PLAY

1. You play on this page, and your friend plays on page 39. So you both need to hold this page up between you to hide your shots.

2. Draw your Defenders anywhere on your field (the one marked HERE). Draw in three Defender 90s (one square), two Defender 110s (two squares) and two Defender 130 Double Cabs (three squares). They can drive horizontally or vertically.

3. Take turns to fire shots over the page at each other's field. You fire by saying which square you're aiming at – 'C6', for instance. Your opponent says 'miss' or 'hit – Defender 90' for instance.

4. Mark your shots on the other field, marked THERE. Put a cross if you hit a Defender and a circle if you miss.

5. Mark your opponent's shots on your HERE field. When a Defender gets wiped out, you have to say 'you destroyed my Defender 90' or whatever.

6. The first person to destroy all seven of the other person's Defenders is the winner, obviously. Duh!

Top Gear loves the Defender! It's an almost indestructible machine that Land Rover made for nearly seventy years, until they sadly killed it off in 2016. It may be disappearing from farms, fields and country roads but it's not forgotten – and thanks to *Top Gear* you can still have fun with it! Find a friend and see who's best at trying to destroy a Defender!

You will need
An opponent

A pen, or a pencil if you want to rub out your drawings and crosses and play again.

DON'T FANCY A FERRARI?

Here are a few other things you could buy if, for some unknown reason, you didn't want to spend £250,000 on a Ferrari . . .

About 800 Xbox One consoles.

One hundred 55-inch curved TVs – perfect for watching *Top Gear*!

ADMIT 500
0414273   0414273

Enough tickets to take 500 friends to the cinema every day for nearly two months! (Don't sit in the posh seats, though.)

1/370th of Luis Suarez. Careful, he may bite more than the puppies!

A month's stay in the biggest apartment at the Ritz Hotel in London. With a butler. And extra champagne.

Eleven Ford Fiesta STs.

400 Miniature Schnauzer puppies

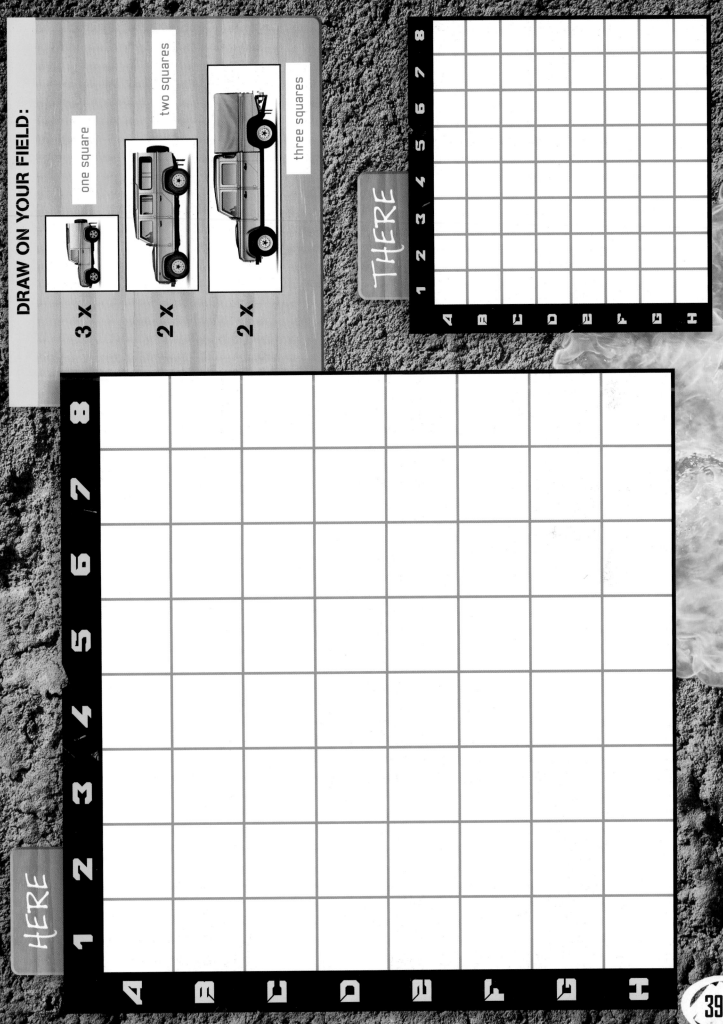

DRAW ON YOUR FIELD:

one square

two squares

three squares

3 x

2 x

2 x

THERE

HERE

39

STIGWATCH

TEENAGE STIG

APPEARANCE
Baggy waistband to show off his pants, headphones, mobile welded to his fist

HABITAT
Shelsley Walsh Speed Hill Climb, Worcestershire

SOME SAY
'What a dismal spectacle.'

AFRICAN STIG

APPEARANCE
Lean and imposing, dressed for a hot climate

HABITAT
A small village in north-eastern Botswana, near the Makgadikgadi Pan

SOME SAY
'He's seen The Lion King 1780 times, and his second-best friend is a Cape buffalo.'

BIG STIG

APPEARANCE
Plus-sized. Generously upholstered. Fat.

HABITAT
Palm Beach International Raceway, Florida

SOME SAY
'He's a CIA experiment that went wrong, and he only eats cheese.'

RIG STIG

APPEARANCE
Burly, beefy, and with one tanned arm from leaning out of the cab window all day

HABITAT
Millbrook Vehicle Proving Grounds, Bedfordshire. Rig Stig can do doughnuts in a truck.

SOME SAY
'His favourite all-time tune is "Forever Autumn" by Justin Hayward.'

Keeping track of the Stig's extensive family can be tricky! Use this handy guide to spot the various types.

GREEN STIG

APPEARANCE
Sandals with socks, solar panels on the helmet and green overalls

HABITAT
MIRA Proving Grounds, Warwickshire

/////// SOME SAY ///////
'His name is Janet Stig-Porter.'

GERMAN STIG

APPEARANCE
Almost identical to the original, except for the presence of a mullet haircut peeping out of his helmet

HABITAT
EuroSpeedway Lausitz, eastern Germany

/////// SOME SAY ///////
'I think it might be Stiggy Ray Cyrus.'

ITALIAN STIG

APPEARANCE
Very sharp, in a smart grey suit with a black shirt and tie, and a little leather man-bag

HABITAT
A huge luxury mobile home parked at the Grand Prix track at Imola

/////// SOME SAY ///////
'What's he been doing? Playing Poker?'

STIG'S CHINESE COUSIN

APPEARANCE
Identical to the original, but much fightier. Sound effects of whacks follow his every move.

HABITAT
A picturesque racetrack on the outskirts of Beijing, China

/////// SOME SAY ///////
'Driving is his second-favourite thing. What's his favourite thing? Attacking people.'

ASTON MARTIN VULCAN
FIRE-BREATHING MONSTER

About three minutes and 24 seconds after Aston built the last £1.2 million One-77 hypercar, some bright spark at the company had the idea to create an even quicker, even louder and even more expensive speed machine. And one that could flame-grill a burger at 200 mph!

Look at that massive rear spoiler, the huge front splitter and those lethal side exhausts. But look quickly, because the Vulcan will zoom past your eyes quicker than, well, just about everything else. It screams speed and power from every corner of its carbon bodywork.

The Vulcan is the fastest, most powerful, most extreme Aston Martin ever built!

The Vulcan's enormous engine is lifted from the Vantage GT3 and magically modified to chuck out 820 bhp – nearly the same as having two V8 Vantages under the front bonnet.

VULCAN'S VITAL STATS

Power: 820 bhp
Engine: 6.0-litre V12
0-60mph: 3 seconds
Top speed: 200 mph+
Price: £1.8 million
Weight: 1,350 kgs
Number made: 24

In the right tunnel, the Vulcan could drive upside down at 190 mph and stick itself to the ceiling. Something to do with aerodynamics and downforce, apparently. Nothing to do with witchcraft.

OMG!

The ancient Roman god of fire and volcanoes was called Vulcan. Aston named this fire-breathing track beast Vulcan. Makes sense, doesn't it?

The exhausts spit flames and the cabin looks like a cross between a fighter jet's cockpit and a spaceship. Off-the-planet stuff!

THE GREAT

Top Gear loves a V8 engine. It's loud, aggressive, powerful . . . and just a little bit pointless, these days. Modern engines can be smaller, lighter and more efficient. But no one's ever going to get nostalgic about a 1.2-litre EcoFlex diesel engine, are they?

Lotus Esprit 1996

Gumpert Apollo

All these cars had (or have) a great V8 under the bonnet. Squeeze them into the big V opposite – there's only one way to fit them all in.

8 letters
JAGUAR XK
ROVER SD1
ZENVO ST1

9 letters
ARIEL ATOM
ASCARI A10

10 letters
RADICAL SR8
TVR CERBERA
PORSCHE 928

11 letters
LANCIA THEMA
LOTUS ESPRIT
TRIUMPH STAG
FORD MUSTANG

13 letters
AUDI V8 QUATTRO
BOWLER WILDCAT
GUMPERT APOLLO
KOENIGSEGG CCX
RENAULT MAGNUM
(yes, it's a truck but we like it)
VAUXHALL MALOO

15 letters
FORD THUNDERBIRD
RANGE ROVER SPORT

16 letters
FERRARI 458 ITALIA

17 letters
CHEVROLET CORVETTE
LAMBORGHINI URRACO

18 letters
LAND ROVER DISCOVERY
MERCEDES-BENZ E63 AMG

20 letters
ASTON MARTIN V8 VANTAGE
BENTLEY CONTINENTAL GT

21 letters
ROLLS-ROYCE SILVER CLOUD

Start with the cars that can only fit in one place – and ignore any dashes in the names!

Bentley Continental GT

Aston Martin V8 Vantage

Koenigsegg CCX

Rolls Royce Silver Cloud

Chevrolet Corvette

45

FILL STIG'S GARAGE

The tame racing driver has a secret underground garage beneath the *Top Gear* test track where he keeps his favourite cars. (This may not actually be true, but wouldn't it be cool?) There are six different cars, in six different colours, parked in a circle. Can you work out from the clues which car is parked where, and what colour it is?

CLUES

1 The orange car is parked opposite the BAC Mono.

2 The silver car is parked opposite the Lamborghini.

3 The Lamborghini is between the blue and orange cars.

4 The red car is parked opposite the Huayra. The red car is also next to the silver car and to the right of the orange car, if it's facing into the circle.

5 The Nissan is parked next to the BAC Mono and opposite the black car.

6 The McLaren is opposite the white car.

CARS

BAC Mono

Ferrari 458 Italia

Lamborghini Aventador

McLaren MP4-12C

Nissan GT-R

Pagani Huayra

COLOURS

- 🔴 Red
- ⚪ White
- 🔵 Blue
- 🟠 Orange
- ⚫ Black
- ⚪ Silver

Orange
McLaren MP4-12C

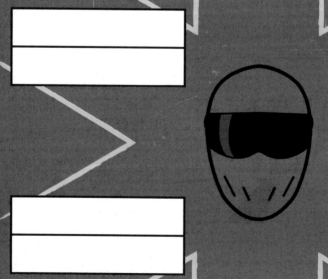

46

Ford Mustang Fastback

Chris reviews the McLAREN 675LT

On a cold day at the *Top Gear* track, Chris gets all hot and bothered about the magnificent McLaren 675LT!

This car is ridiculous!

Eagled-eye readers will spot this isn't a 675LT. It's the McLaren F1 GTR, which was built in the 1990s and labelled the Long Tail. Chris loves its speed.

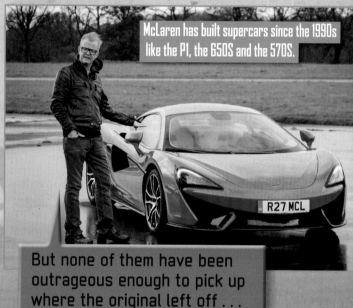

McLaren has built supercars since the 1990s like the P1, the 650S and the 570S.

R27 MCL

But none of them have been outrageous enough to pick up where the original left off . . .

. . . until now!

LT03 MCL

Chris then gets inside the 675LT. The first McLaren to take the Long Tail (LT) name since that F1.

Zero to sixty in 2.8 seconds!

He is very, very, very impressed.

He takes the 675LT to an amazing 200 mph.

That's the fastest I have ever been in a car!

The LT's super speed is helped by it being a very lightweight machine.

This car is 100 kgs lighter than the 650. The carbon fibre seats save 15 kgs.

All this weight saving and racing technology makes the McLaren ultra quick in the corners.

Hammerhead has never been so fun!

Formula One driver Jenson Button pops along to show Chris what the car will *really* do.

With the traction control off, Chris has a quiet word with Button behind the wheel.

This is *amazing* fun!

Back in the seat, Chris has nothing but praise for this £259,500 supercar.

Be careful! You don't want to go on the . . . GRASS!!!

The 675LT really does live up to the Long Tail name.

Comparing it to the F1, he says it could become one of the best McLarens ever.

Then the Stig takes the 675LT for a power lap around the *Top Gear* track.

The result is brilliant, and maybe even legendary.

Chris reveals the 675LT's Power Lap time . . .

McLaren 675LT

Power: 666 bhp
Engine: 3.8-litre twin turbo V8
0-60 mph: 2.8 seconds
Top speed: 205 mph
Price: £259,500

It's a brand new record! Well done, McLaren!

McLaren 675LT	1:13.7
PAGANI HUAYRA	1:13.8
MONO	4.3
ATOM	
LAMBORGHIN	
MP4-12C	1:16.2

MAD CARS

Ford Fiestas, Vauxhall Insignias and Volvo S80s are all very well, but they're not interesting. They're not fun. Sometimes you just want to gawp at totally bonkers cars and say 'huh'? That's where *Top Gear* comes in . . .

Lamborghini Egoista

Built to celebrate Lambo's fiftieth birthday, you have to ask what the Italians thought was going to happen at the party. You see, the Egoista is made from anti-radar, stealth-seeking, jet-fighter carbon fibre – did they think aliens would attack their celebrations and steal the sausage rolls? It's mad and bad, but we're glad it exists!

Avtoros Shaman

It's Russian. It has a bed inside. It has eight gigantic wheels. It will crush anything on the road. It will crush anything on a mountain. It even has a propeller to blast it along in the water. The Avtoros Shaman is totally, totally ridiculous! We love it.

Maybach Exelero

The world's fastest, most expensive and most ludicrous limousine is the Maybach Exelero. Let's look at the numbers – 700 bhp, 217 mph, 0-60 mph in four seconds, 2.7 tonnes and six metres long. Only one was ever made and it sold for £5.5 million a few years back. It's so wrong, but so right.

Caparo T1 police car

Those nice people at Caparo created a special version of its Formula One-inspired T1 speed machine – a 'car' that will do 0-60 mph in 2.5 seconds and reach 200 mph – for British cops. Only one problem – it's a single seater and has no room to take the crims to jail.

Mercedes G63 AMG 6x6

This is the maddest road-going Merc ever. It's also at home on 600-ft sand dunes, snow-covered mountains and one metre-deep lakes. The madness doesn't stop there – check out the six 37-inch wheels, the 5.5-litre twin-turbo V8 engine and the £370,000 price tag.

Tumbler

Batman doesn't mess about. When the world's darkest superhero needed a mean and moody new Batmobile for the *Dawn of Justice* movie, he created a machine so scary it could eat a Land Rover for lunch. The Tumbler is an awesome armour-plated V8 beast. Small children are advised not to even look at this picture.

51

Lamborghini Egoista

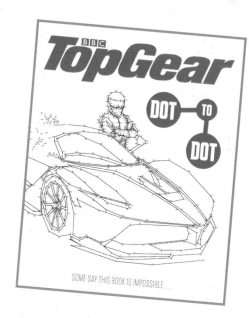

SOME SAY THIS BOOK IS IMPOSSIBLE...

Join the dots to reveal
who's hidden on this page!

Top Gear Dot-To-Dot is out
in November and contains
over forty-five tricky
dot-to-dot puzzles!

What's Your *Top Gear* Nickname?

Lots of cars have nicknames. A Ferrari is called a Fezza, a Subaru is known as a Scooby and a Daihatsu is called a Rust Bucket. We may have made one of these up. But what would your *Top Gear* nickname be? Follow these rules to find out . . .

1 Look for your birthdate to find the first name in your nickname:

1	Tailpipe
2	Dipstick
3	Bucket Seat
4	Kit Kat
5	Powered
6	Torque
7	Wideload
8	Aero
9	Chequered
10	Rotary
11	Gasoline
12	Wing Nut
13	Dangerous
14	Smokin'
15	Carbon Fibre
16	Sideways
17	Master
18	Turbocharged
19	Checkpoint
20	Top End
21	Flappy Paddle
22	Wrench
23	Rocket-powered
24	Buckle Up
25	Pitstop
26	Speedy
27	One Way
28	Thirsty
29	Clutch
30	Rally Faced
31	Octane

2 Now discover the second part of your nickname, taken from the month you were born:

January	Sniffer
February	Beans
March	Loon
April	Cruncher
May	Charlie
June	Trousers
July	Overspill
August	The Great
September	Pork Pie
October	Winklepicker
November	Spoiler
December	Roger

Top Gear Top Tip

If you're posh and have a double-barreled surname, or something silly like 'Le' in the middle of your name, then think of a daft word to replace it with.

Matt's Mad Tour

Matt Le Blanc is 'enjoying' his crazy tour of London with Ken Block behind the wheel, but can you spot ten differences between the pictures below?

TRACK TIME

The headline says it all – it's time to build your own *Top Gear* track. Straight bits, corners, bendy bits, bumpy bits . . . you'll need them all to keep the Stig happy!

Add a chicane?

Wave to the spectators here?

THINGS NEEDED FOR A TOP GEAR TRACK . . .

· A start
· A finish*
· Grass (for celebs to drive through)
· A jumbo jet in the background
· Tarmac (Stig can't burn rubber on sand, can he?)

* Usually where the start is.

Slow down for a hairpin?

Come on, baby!

Reach top speed here?

Will your *Top Gear* track have an off-road bit? We recommend only taking the Rally-cross Mini over this bit. A £1 million Pagani may get a bit dusty, and a bit busted, here.

Flat out through the corner?

Hairpin

Jump

Start/finish

Gambon

Watersplash

Tyre wall

Hammerhead

57

EVERYTHING MUST GO!

Round the back of the *Top Gear* studio is a huge pile of random stuff that we need to get rid of. It's taking up loads of room and is available for a reasonable price. Actually, it's available for any price if you take it off our hands . . .

Reliant Rialto

Missing door. And roof. Rather dirty and wet. Abandoned on a hillside near Blackpool.

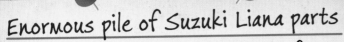

Shredded Mini Tyres

Quite a few of these. The celebs seem to enjoy making smoke, mud and water fly from them.

Ice Cream Van

Last seen being pulled along Blackpool beach by a Jeep, so the Cornettos could be a bit water damaged.

Enormous pile of Suzuki Liana parts

At least two gearboxes, many wheels, front and rear bumpers, hubcaps, etc. Probably all broken but might be something there. Free if buyer collects.

600 office water cooler bottles (empty)

Many broken and cracked, the rest scratched following a massive collision.

Old sheepskin coat

Matt dumped this after he got back from Blackpool. It looks about 43 years old, and smells like 43-year-old mouldy cheese.

Skirting from a Merc GLC

Eddie took the Merc off-road without putting it in off-road mode. He then ripped bits of bodywork from it. Not that he worried too much!

London A-Z

Matt and his American mate Ken left it behind after their trip around London. Ken didn't really use it much.

3,000 tonnes of topsoil

Some guys dug a big hole next to the TG track and filled it with water. As a result there's a LOT of earth going spare, if you're interested.

More Shredded Tyres

We think these belonged to a Mr K. Block. He rather enjoys the smell of burning rubber by the looks of it!

Used helmets

The new owner needs to like the Stars and Stripes or the Union Jack. Plenty of mud and sand to be cleaned off first, though.

Fun-ometer 3000

Chris Harris wore this strange headgear to 'scientifically' prove the BMW M2 is a fun car on the Top Gear track. It doesn't look very scientific though and was probably made by a three-year old at playschool.

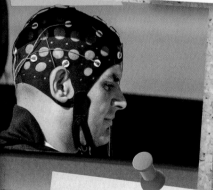

Sick Bags

Sabine ordered a job lot of these after her driving caused several passengers (including Chris) to lose their lunch.

ANSWERS

PAGES 44-45:
THE GREAT V8

(Word search answer grid)

PAGE 46:
FILL STIG'S GARAGE

Follow the clues in this order to park the cars: 1, 4, 3, 5, 2, 6. Then the red car must be the Ferrari. Clockwise the cars are:

Orange McLaren MP4-12C
Black Lamborghini Aventador
Blue Pagani Huayra
White BAC Mono
Silver Nissan GT-R
Red Ferrari 458 Italia.

PAGE 33:
HURACÁN OR HUAYRA?

Citroën Cactus
Fiat Ulysse
Ford Probe
Honda Freed Spike
Hyundai Accent
Isuzu Bighorn Plaisir
Kia pro_cee'd
Mazda Bongo Friendee
Mercedes Vaneo
Mitsubishi Toppo Guppy
Nissan Cube
Proton Savvy
Renault Wind
Skoda Roomster
Suzuki Wagon R
Toyota Chaser Lordly
Vauxhall Adam Slam
Volkswagen Routan

PAGE 55:
MATT'S MAD TOUR